Fractions

AGE 9-11

Dr Bill Gillham

As a parent, you can play a major role in your child's education by your interest and encouragement. This book will help to improve your child's grasp of the vital mathematical concept of fractions. It is designed to:

- teach and test your child's progress and understanding
- teach the concept of the fraction, not just the arithmetic of it
- teach the principles of computation in fractions and decimal fractions in a way that leads to understanding
- teach the relationship between ordinary fractions and decimal fractions
- help them to understand how fractions work in real-life situations

This book is divided into two sections: fractions and decimal fractions. The first section contains 13 tests; the second section 10 tests. There is also an end-of-book test and rating chart. The whole book is a month's work programme.

Hodder Children's Books

The only home learning programme supported by the NCPTA

How to help your child

- Don't expect children to do more than one test a day.

- Make sure they can read and understand the instructions.

- Explain they can't use a calculator (unless the test says so!)

- Tell them to ask for help: show them how to do the problem but let them work out the answer for themselves.

- Encourage your child to record daily progress on the bar graphs at the beginning of each section.

- The tests are carefully graded but if your child scores fewer than eight on a test then they have not mastered the test material. Go through the errors, explaining the working and then make up similar examples until they have the idea.

- Go over any mistakes *briefly* pointing out where they have gone wrong.

- Use plenty of praise. Children thrive on success!

Published by Hodder Children's Books 1995

10 9 8

All rights reserved. No part of this publication may be reproduced, stored in a retrieval system, or transmitted, in any form or by any means, without the prior written permission of the publisher, nor be otherwise circulated in any form of binding or cover other than that in which it is published and without a similar condition being imposed on the subsequent purchaser.

ISBN 0 340 65111 3

Copyright © WEC Gillham 1984

The right of Dr. Bill Gillham to be identified as the author of the Work has been asserted by him in accordance with the Copyright, Designs and Patents Act 1988.

Printed and bound in Great Britain

Hodder Children's Books
A division of Hodder Headline plc
338 Euston Road
London NW1 3BH

Previously published as Test Your Child's Fractions and Decimal Fractions

CHECK YOUR PROGRESS
Fractions (pages 4 – 17)

Record your progress on this bar graph.
Shade in for each test.

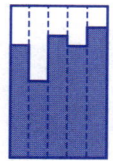

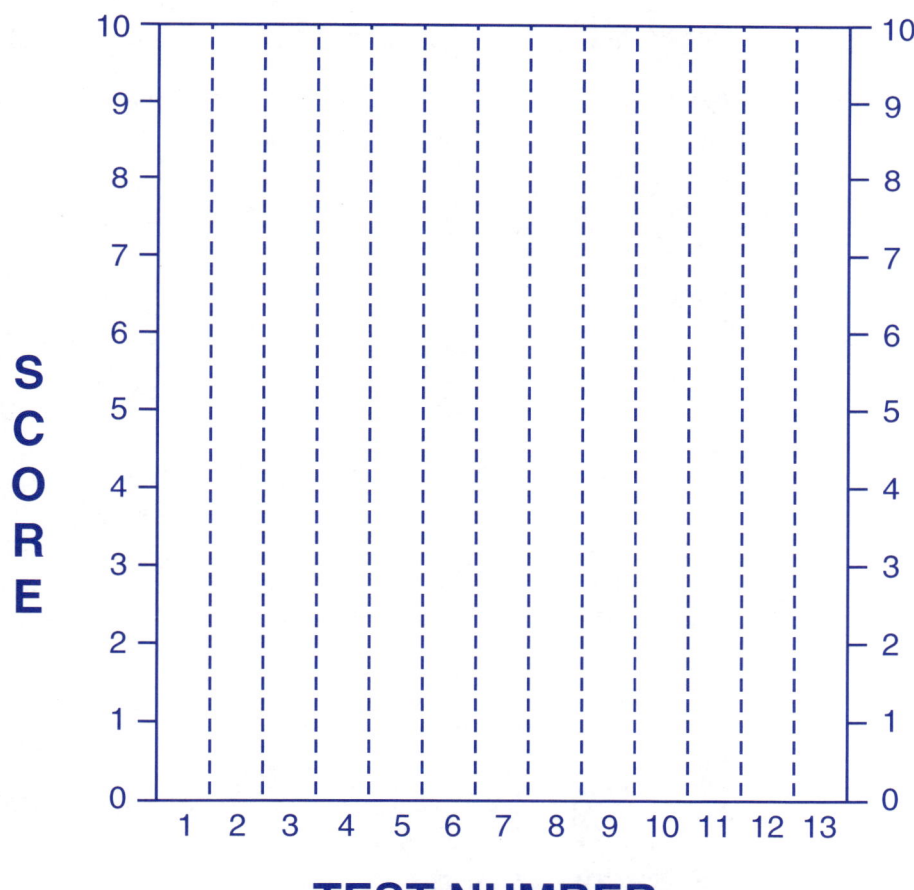

Fractions: the basics

We start with a whole

A fraction is *part* of a whole

It may be a big part or it may be a small part

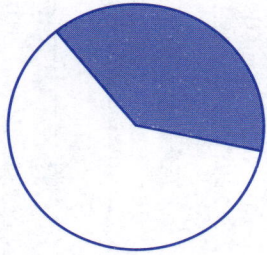 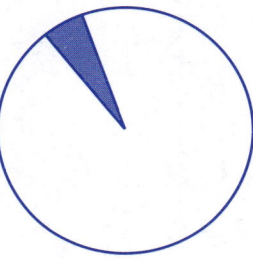

Ordinary fractions are written like this: $\frac{3}{4}$ ← **numerator**
← **denominator**

- The **numerator** tells you how many parts there are in the fraction.
- The **denominator** tells you how many *equal* parts the whole is divided into.

Here is a square (a whole) divided into four equal parts:

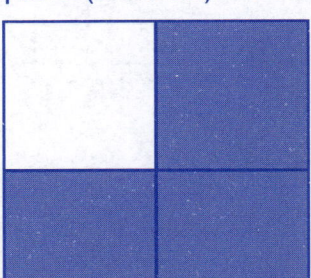

What fraction is shaded in?
3 of the 4 equal parts are shaded in so the fraction is:

$$\frac{3}{4}$$

Now turn to test 1

Test 1

1  How many parts are shaded in? ———▶ ___
How many parts is the square divided into? ——▶

2  How many parts are shaded in? ———▶ ___
How many parts is the triangle divided into? ——▶

See how you do it? Good! Now write the fractions shaded in for these.

3 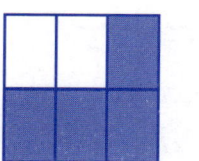 = ——

4 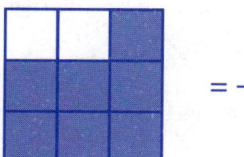 = ——

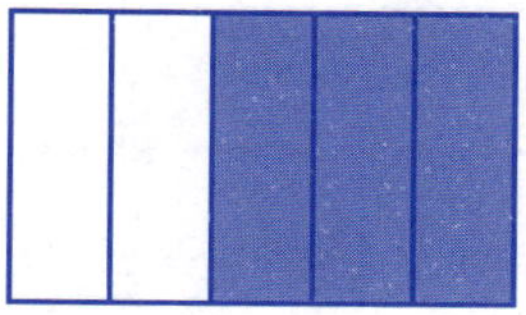

5 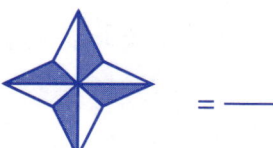 = ——

6  = ——

7 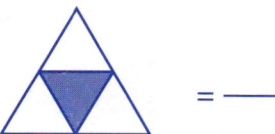 = ——

8 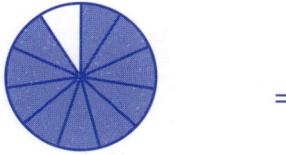 = ——

9 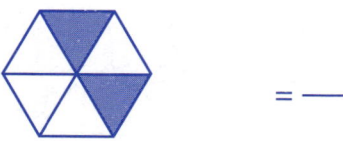 = ——

10 = ——

Score = | 10 |

Test 2

1 Shade in $\frac{1}{4}$ of this square

2 Shade in $\frac{1}{3}$ of this square

3 Shade in $\frac{5}{6}$ of this rectangle

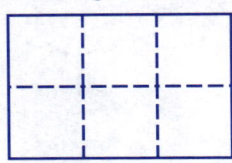

4 Shade in $\frac{4}{5}$ of this shape

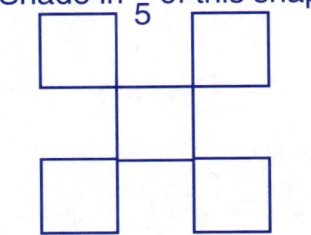

5 Shade in $\frac{7}{8}$ of this rectangle

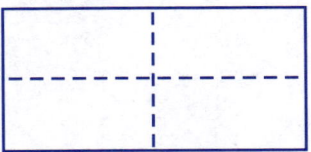

6 Shade in $\frac{1}{2}$ of this triangle

7 Shade in $\frac{3}{4}$ of this circle

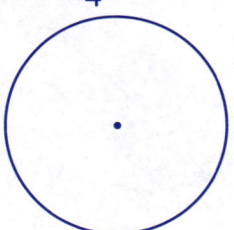

8 Shade in $\frac{1}{5}$ of this polygon

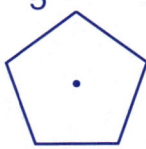

9 Shade in $\frac{8}{8}$ of this circle

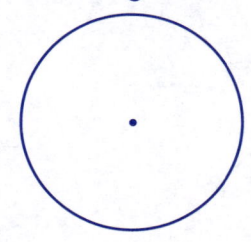

10 Shade in $\frac{2}{3}$ of this shape

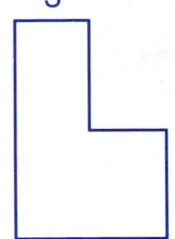

	10

Test 3
Fractions: just a part of something

A fraction is part of a whole: it can be a big whole or a very little one (a quarter of a million pounds is a lot more than a quarter of 10p, for example)

Try the first one of these and then ask a grown-up to check your answer before you go on.

1 A
   B   What fraction of B is A? ____

2 A
   B   What fraction of B is A? ____

3 A
   B   What fraction of B is A? ____

4 A
   B   What fraction of B is A? ____

5 A
   B   What fraction of B is A? ____

6 A
   B   What fraction of B is A? ____

7 A
   B   What fraction of C is A? ____
8 C   What fraction of B is A? ____

9 A
   B   What fraction of C is A? ____
10 C   What fraction of C is B? ____

10

Test 4

If we cut something into 100 equal pieces and give someone 50 of them we would have given them $\frac{50}{100}$ of the whole. But you can write the fraction more simply by reducing it to its lowest terms. When you give $\frac{50}{100}$ of the whole you give $\frac{1}{2}$ of the whole

The answer is simple: you divide the numerator and denominator by the biggest number that will go into both. 50 goes into 100 (twice) and into 50 (once) so:

$$\frac{\cancel{50}^{1}}{\cancel{100}_{2}} = \frac{1}{2}$$

This is called cancelling down. See if you can cancel these down to their lowest terms

1. $\frac{6}{12} = $ ——   2. $\frac{3}{9} = $ ——

3. $\frac{15}{20} = $ ——   4. $\frac{4}{16} = $ ——

5. $\frac{9}{12} = $ ——   6. $\frac{16}{24} = $ ——

7. $\frac{18}{20} = $ ——   8. $\frac{8}{10} = $ ——

9. $\frac{14}{49} = $ ——   10. $\frac{4}{40} = $ ——

Test 5

Everyday fractions

We use fractions every day of our lives

1. If you have 12 felt-tip pens and lose a quarter of them, how many do you have left?

2. If there are 28 children in your class and three-quarters of them are going on a school trip, how many children are *not* going?

3. How much does half a kilo of potatoes cost if they are 92p a kilo?

4. If you do this test and get only three-fifths of the questions right, how many do you get wrong?

5. You have a bag of 45 sweets. You give your sister a third of them: how many do you have left?

6. If a round fruit cake is cut into quarters and then each quarter is cut into quarters again, how many people can have a piece?

7. In a sale the price of a model kit is reduced by a fifth. The sale price is £4. What was the original price?

8. Your height now is 1 metre 60 centimetres, yet two years ago you were only seven-eighths of that height. How tall were you then?

9. If you plant 36 crocus bulbs but one twelfth of them don't grow, how many flowers do you end up with?

10. Your aunt sends you a £5 note, which includes 50p for your little brother. What fraction of the £5 is his?

Test 6

Clock fractions

Do you realise that there are fractions on a clock face? All the way round is a whole one (an hour), anything less is a fraction. To make it easier for you the fraction clock only has a minute hand. You draw in the minute hand to show the fraction given

Remember! A minute is $\frac{1}{60}$ of an hour, so five minutes is $\frac{1}{12}$ of an hour.

Example

$= \frac{1}{2}$

1. $= \frac{1}{4}$
2. $= \frac{3}{4}$
3. $= \frac{1}{3}$
4. $= \frac{1}{12}$
5. $= \frac{5}{6}$
6. $= \frac{11}{12}$
7. $= \frac{2}{3}$
8. $= \frac{1}{6}$
9. $= \frac{7}{12}$
10. $= \frac{1}{24}$

Test 7

Odd man out!

Which of these fractions is different from the rest?

$\frac{500}{1000}$ $\frac{27}{54}$ $\frac{9}{18}$ $\frac{8}{14}$ $\frac{111}{222}$

The answer is $\frac{8}{14}$. All the rest are different ways of writing $\frac{1}{2}$ when they are cancelled down. Put a ring round the 'odd man out' in these. All but one of them is the same as the 'lowest terms' fraction in the box at the end

1	$\frac{4}{12}$	$\frac{30}{90}$	$\frac{200}{400}$	$\frac{125}{375}$	$\frac{15}{45}$	$\frac{1}{3}$
2	$\frac{25}{100}$	$\frac{3}{12}$	$\frac{30}{120}$	$\frac{16}{64}$	$\frac{9}{40}$	$\frac{1}{4}$
3	$\frac{3}{15}$	$\frac{11}{45}$	$\frac{7}{35}$	$\frac{8}{40}$	$\frac{50}{250}$	$\frac{1}{5}$
4	$\frac{30}{240}$	$\frac{7}{56}$	$\frac{9}{64}$	$\frac{5}{40}$	$\frac{4}{32}$	$\frac{1}{8}$
5	$\frac{9}{12}$	$\frac{16}{24}$	$\frac{66}{99}$	$\frac{200}{300}$	$\frac{18}{27}$	$\frac{2}{3}$
6	$\frac{4}{24}$	$\frac{2}{15}$	$\frac{5}{30}$	$\frac{12}{72}$	$\frac{7}{42}$	$\frac{1}{6}$
7	$\frac{15}{20}$	$\frac{75}{100}$	$\frac{9}{12}$	$\frac{20}{24}$	$\frac{6}{8}$	$\frac{3}{4}$
8	$\frac{10}{100}$	$\frac{6}{72}$	$\frac{8}{96}$	$\frac{20}{240}$	$\frac{3}{36}$	$\frac{1}{12}$
9	$\frac{12}{24}$	$\frac{65}{130}$	$\frac{140}{260}$	$\frac{44}{88}$	$\frac{5}{10}$	$\frac{1}{2}$
10	$\frac{8}{20}$	$\frac{20}{45}$	$\frac{12}{30}$	$\frac{40}{100}$	$\frac{14}{35}$	$\frac{2}{5}$

10

Test 8

Addition of fractions: 1

To add fractions you have to have the denominators the same:

$$\frac{1}{5} + \frac{3}{5} = \frac{4}{5}$$

You add the numerators not the denominators.

But what do you do if the denominators are *not* the same? For example:

$$\frac{1}{5} + \frac{3}{10}$$

You have to give them the same denominator.

STEP ONE

Step one

$$\frac{}{10}$$

Find the lowest number *both* denominators will go into; both 5 and 10 will go into 10, so draw a long line with 10 underneath.

STEP TWO

Step two

$$\frac{(2\times1) + (1\times3)}{10}$$

Multiply the numerator of each fraction by the number of times the *denominator* will go into this 'lowest common denominator'. In $\frac{1}{5}$ the 5 goes into 10 twice, so we multiply the numerator by two; in $\frac{3}{10}$ the 10 goes into 10 once (of course) so we multiply the numerator by one.

$$= \frac{2+3}{10} = \frac{5}{10}$$

which cancels down to $\frac{1}{2}$.

Now do these for practice.

1. $\frac{1}{8} + \frac{3}{8} =$ 2. $\frac{2}{9} + \frac{5}{9} =$

3. $\frac{2}{3} + \frac{1}{6} =$ 4. $\frac{1}{2} + \frac{1}{8} =$

5. $\frac{1}{4} + \frac{1}{6} =$ 6. $\frac{3}{10} + \frac{3}{5} =$

7. $\frac{1}{5} + \frac{1}{3} =$ 8. $\frac{1}{3} + \frac{1}{7} =$

9. $\frac{3}{4} + \frac{1}{6} =$ 10. $\frac{8}{15} + \frac{2}{5} =$

	10

Test 9

Addition of fractions: 2

Example $\frac{3}{4} + \frac{2}{3} = \frac{9+8}{12} = \frac{17}{12} = 1\frac{5}{12}$

1. $\frac{1}{2} + \frac{2}{3} =$
2. $\frac{1}{4} + \frac{7}{8} =$
3. $\frac{7}{9} + \frac{2}{3} =$
4. $\frac{1}{2} + \frac{3}{5} =$
5. $\frac{1}{3} + \frac{11}{12} =$

Example $1\frac{3}{4} + 1\frac{1}{3} = 2\frac{9+4}{12} = 2\frac{13}{12} = 3\frac{1}{12}$

1. $2\frac{3}{5} + 1\frac{1}{5} =$
2. $3\frac{5}{8} + 2\frac{1}{4} =$
3. $1\frac{5}{9} + 2\frac{2}{3} =$
4. $2\frac{2}{3} + 4\frac{1}{2} =$
5. $4\frac{11}{12} + \frac{1}{6} =$

10

Test 10

Subtraction of fractions: 1

When you take one fraction away from another you also have to make the denominators the same. So, if you start with:

$$\frac{3}{4} - \frac{1}{6}$$ you have to change it to:

$$= \frac{(3 \times 3) - (2 \times 1)}{12}$$ then you subtract the second *numerator* from the first one, $= \frac{9-2}{12} = \frac{7}{12}$

Now try these:

1. $\frac{3}{5} - \frac{2}{5} =$

2. $\frac{5}{6} - \frac{1}{3} =$

3. $\frac{7}{8} - \frac{1}{2} =$

4. $\frac{2}{3} - \frac{3}{9} =$

5. $\frac{5}{14} - \frac{1}{7} =$

6. $\frac{3}{8} - \frac{1}{16} =$

7. $\frac{3}{5} - \frac{3}{8} =$

8. $\frac{6}{7} - \frac{1}{3} =$

9. $\frac{1}{8} - \frac{1}{12} =$

10. $\frac{3}{5} - \frac{1}{4} =$

Test 11

Subtraction of fractions: 2

When you subtract a larger fraction from a smaller fraction and a whole number, you have to borrow from the whole number. Like this:

$$2\tfrac{1}{8} - \tfrac{3}{8} = 1\tfrac{9}{8} - \tfrac{3}{8} = 1\tfrac{6}{8} = 1\tfrac{3}{4}$$

Now try these:

1. $3\tfrac{1}{3} - \tfrac{2}{3} =$

2. $1\tfrac{1}{2} - \tfrac{3}{4} =$

3. $1\tfrac{5}{8} - \tfrac{3}{4} =$

4. $1\tfrac{1}{3} - \tfrac{1}{2} =$

5. $3\tfrac{3}{8} - \tfrac{7}{8} =$

6. $2\tfrac{3}{5} - \tfrac{7}{10} =$

7. $4\tfrac{1}{4} - \tfrac{1}{2} =$

8. $1\tfrac{7}{12} - \tfrac{11}{12} =$

9. $3\tfrac{1}{9} - \tfrac{1}{3} =$

10. $5\tfrac{1}{2} - \tfrac{5}{7} =$

Test 12

Multiplication of fractions

You just multiply the numerators and multiply the denominators, and then cancel down if necessary. *Remember*, a fraction times a fraction means that the answer is *always* smaller than either of them

Example

$\frac{1}{8} \times \frac{2}{3} = \frac{2}{24} = \frac{1}{12}$

Got the idea? Right, now try these..

1) $\frac{3}{5} \times \frac{1}{2} =$ 2) $\frac{3}{4} \times \frac{3}{5} =$

3) $\frac{7}{8} \times \frac{1}{3} =$ 4) $\frac{1}{16} \times \frac{1}{2} =$

5) $\frac{7}{9} \times \frac{1}{5} =$ 6) $\frac{3}{8} \times \frac{3}{10} =$

7) $\frac{1}{2} \times \frac{3}{7} =$ 8) $\frac{5}{12} \times \frac{1}{3} =$

9) $\frac{5}{11} \times \frac{2}{9} =$ 10) $\frac{7}{35} \times \frac{1}{2} =$

	10

Test 13

Division of fractions

You just turn the second fraction (the divisor) upside down and multiply. That's all there is to it!

Example

$\frac{1}{2} \div \frac{1}{4} = \frac{1}{2} \times \frac{4}{1} = \frac{4}{2} = 2$

When you divide a fraction by a smaller fraction the answer is *always* bigger than either of the fractions

1. $\frac{3}{4} \div \frac{1}{4} = \frac{3}{4} \times \frac{4}{1} =$

2. $\frac{2}{3} \div \frac{1}{6} =$

3. $\frac{7}{8} \div \frac{1}{2} =$

4. $\frac{3}{5} \div \frac{1}{4} =$

5. $\frac{3}{8} \div \frac{1}{16} =$

6. $\frac{5}{7} \div \frac{2}{3} =$

7. $\frac{6}{11} \div \frac{1}{2} =$

8. $\frac{5}{9} \div \frac{1}{9} =$

9. $\frac{5}{6} \div \frac{1}{3} =$

10. $\frac{1}{4} \div \frac{1}{8} =$

10

CHECK YOUR PROGRESS
Decimal Fractions (pages 19 – 29)

Record your progress on this bar graph.
Shade in for each test.

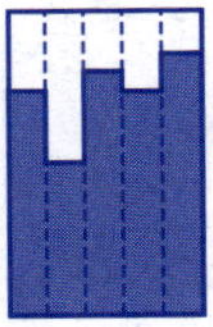

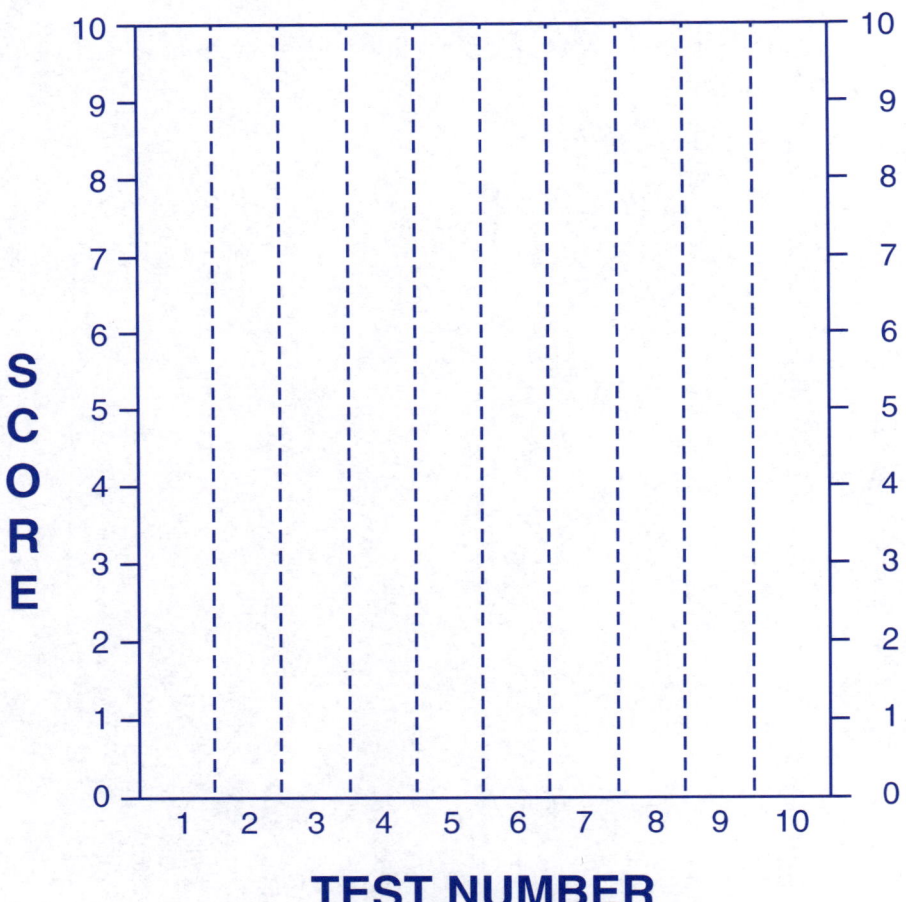

The mighty dot

There is no dot quite so important as the decimal point – its position determines the value of the numbers on either side of it

HERE IT IS

The further numbers go in this direction the bigger they become

The further numbers go in this direction the smaller they become

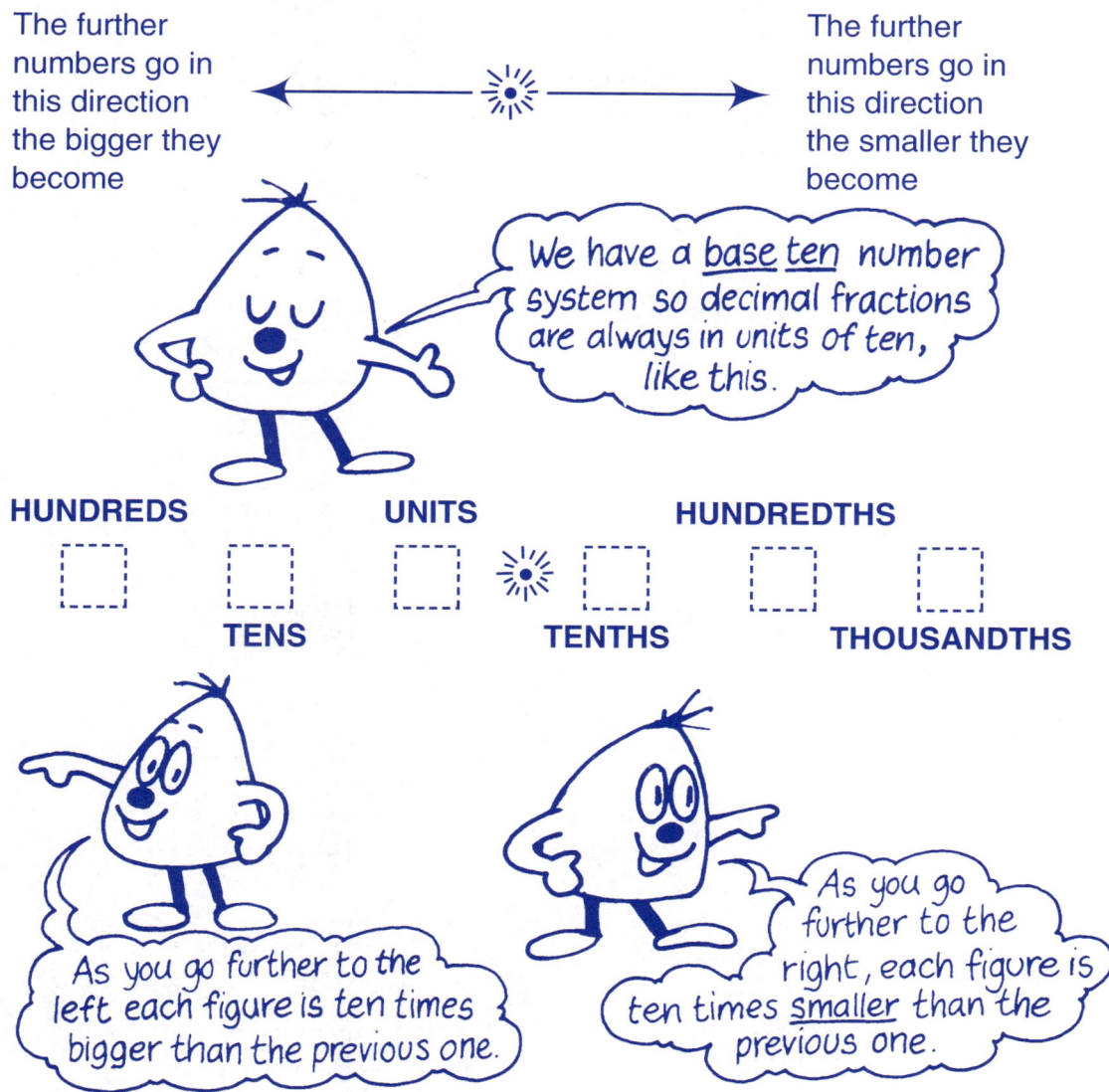

We have a <u>base ten</u> number system so decimal fractions are always in units of ten, like this.

HUNDREDS   UNITS   HUNDREDTHS
TENS   TENTHS   THOUSANDTHS

As you go further to the left each figure is ten times bigger than the previous one.

As you go further to the right, each figure is ten times <u>smaller</u> than the previous one.

We are going to concentrate on the figures to the *right* of the decimal point – the decimal fractions. And we shall only go to three places of decimals – as far as *thousandths*

Now turn to test 1

Test 1

Example

How many tenths in this decimal fraction?   0.363 → 3

Notice how there is always a nought before the decimal point if there are no whole ones. Now try these...

1. How many hundredths?   0.364
2. How many thousandths?   0.364
3. How many tenths?   0.217
4. How many thousandths?   0.718
5. How many tenths?   0.572
6. How many hundredths?   0.282
7. How many thousandths?   0.209
8. How many hundredths?   0.701
9. How many tenths?   0.063
10. How many thousandths?   0.76

10

Test 2

The decimal in your pocket

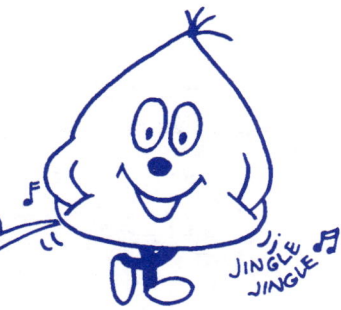

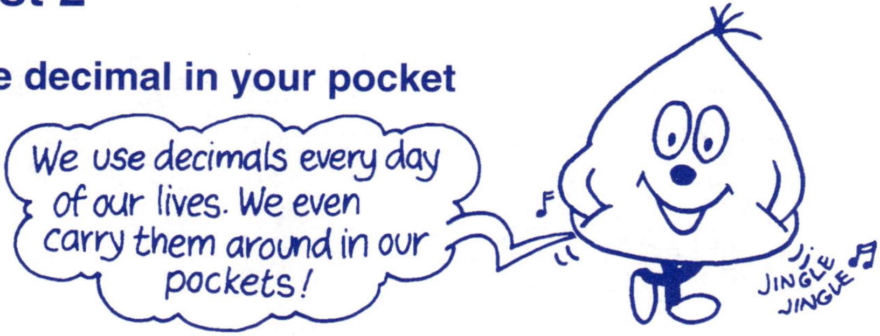
We use decimals every day of our lives. We even carry them around in our pockets!
JINGLE JINGLE

If you have a 1p coin then you have a hundredth (0.01) of a pound. If you have a 10p coin then you have a tenth (0.1) of a pound. If you have a pound then you have a *whole* one (1.0).

Do you get the idea? Right, now express these as decimals of £1. The first two have been done for you

10p + 5p = £0.15

5p + 2p = £0.07

1 10p + 2p = £0.

2 1p + 1p + 1p = £0.

3 20p + 5p = £0.

4 50p + 1p = £0.

5 10p + 10p = £0.

6 20p + 10p + 2p = £0.

7 50p + 10p + 5p = £0.

8 10p + 5p + 2p + 1p = £0.

9 50p + 20p + 10p + 2p = £0.

10 20p + 10p + 5p + 2p = £0.

10

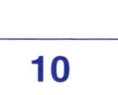

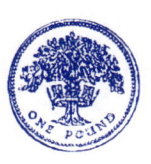

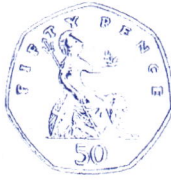

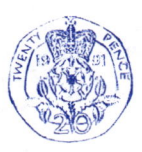

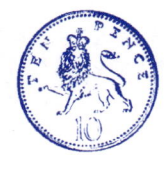

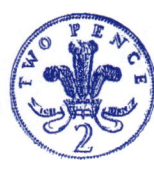

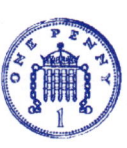

£1.00 £0.50 £0.20 £0.10 £0.05 £0.02 £0.01

Test 3

Using a decimal number line

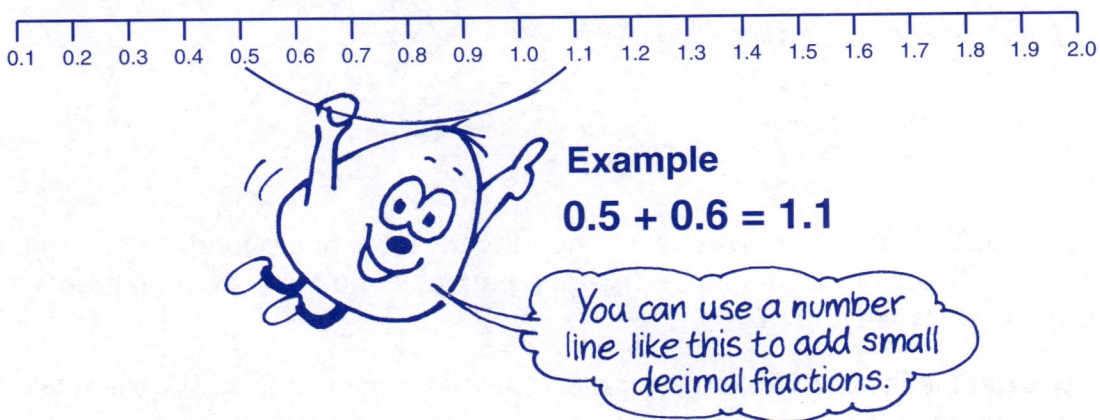

Example
0.5 + 0.6 = 1.1

You can use a number line like this to add small decimal fractions.

See how it's done? Right, now try these, using the number line

1 0.3 + 0.4 =

2 0.6 + 0.6 =

3 0.8 + 0.2 =

4 0.2 + 0.7 =

5 0.4 + 0.8 =

6 0.5 + 0.3 =

7 0.6 + 0.7 =

8 0.9 + 0.3 =

9 0.7 + 0.7 + 0.3 =

10 0.8 + 0.5 + 0.6 =

10

Test 4

Fraction conversion line

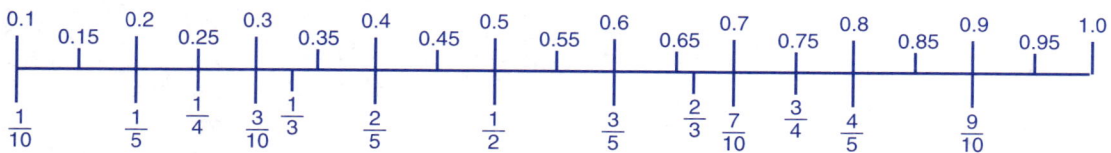

This conversion line matches up decimal fractions and some common ordinary fractions. Perhaps you can see why engineers normally prefer to use decimal fractions – they are all in the same currency. It is simpler to add 0.5 and 0.6 than $\frac{1}{2}$ and $\frac{3}{5}$

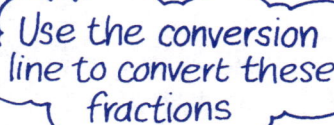

Use the conversion line to convert these fractions

1. $\frac{3}{10}$ =
2. 0.6 =
3. $\frac{1}{4}$ =
4. 0.75 =
5. $\frac{3}{5}$ =
6. 0.4 =
7. $\frac{4}{5}$ =
8. 0.7 =
9. $\frac{1}{3}$ =
10. 0.2 =

10

Test 5

Practical decimals

1 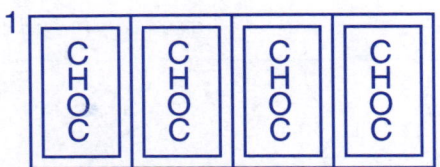 Colour in 0.25 of this bar of chocolate

 I like this one.

2 0.5 of a metre = _____ cm = _____ mm

3  Colour in 0.7 of these stars

4  How many more packets do you need to make a kilogram? Draw them here

5 Two full bottles of washing up liquid make 1 litre. 300ml (millilitres) have been used from the first bottle. What decimal fraction of the litre is left?
0._ _ _ _ _ _ _

6 Here is a box of Christmas crackers. What decimal fraction of the whole box is the cracker shaded in?
0._ _ _ _ _ _ _

7 If you have thirty marbles and you lose 0.3 of them, how many have you lost? (Find 0.1 then times by 3)

8 Your father is two metres tall and you are 0.75 of his height. How tall are you?   _____ m _____ cm

9 What is 0.4 of £2?   _ _ _ _ _ _ _

10 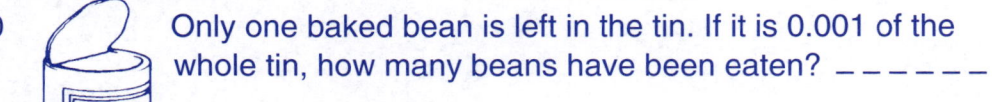 Only one baked bean is left in the tin. If it is 0.001 of the whole tin, how many beans have been eaten? _ _ _ _ _ _ _ _

| 10 |

24

Test 6

Converting decimal fractions into ordinary fractions

- If the decimal is to one place (0.7) it goes over 10 = $\frac{7}{10}$

- If the decimal is to two places (0.75) it goes over 100 = $\frac{75}{100}$

- If the decimal is to three places (0.752) it goes over 1000 = $\frac{752}{1000}$

Now convert these to ordinary fractions (the first one is done for you)

0.215 = $\frac{215}{1000}$

1 0.7   = ———   2 0.26 = ———

3 0.18 = ———   4 0.1   = ———

5 0.78 = ———   6 0.216 = ———

7 0.35 = ———   8 0.8   = ———

9 0.377 = ———   10 0.009 = ———

As an extra see if you can cancel any of them down.

Test 7

Converting ordinary fractions into decimal fractions

- Here is a fraction: $\frac{2}{5}$

- To find the decimal fraction you divide the numerator (2) by the denominator (5) and to do this you have to put a decimal point and a 0 after the 2, like this:

$$\begin{array}{r} 0.4 \\ 5\overline{)2.0} \\ 20 \end{array}$$

You put a decimal point in the answer, too.

- Usually it's best to do these with a calculator (but a calculator won't help you unless you know what to do ...)

Do the first two without a calculator, but use a calculator for the rest – give the whole number answer shown on the calculator.

1. $\frac{1}{4}$ = $4\overline{)1.00}^{\,0.}$ = 0

2. $\frac{5}{8}$ = $8\overline{)5.000}^{\,0.}$ = 0

3. $\frac{9}{20}$ = 0.

4. $\frac{2}{3}$ = 0.

5. $\frac{1}{9}$ = 0.

6. $\frac{5}{6}$ = 0.

7. $\frac{7}{8}$ = 0.

8. $\frac{3}{11}$ = 0.

9. $\frac{19}{20}$ = 0.

10. $\frac{9}{11}$ = 0.

Test 8

Addition of decimal fractions

The rule is: keep your decimal points in line or you'll go wrong. For example:

$$0.732 + 0.9 + 0.35$$

```
 0.732
 0.9
 0.35 +
 1.982
```

To add these you have to set them out vertically like this:

Now set these out and add them up

1. $0.3 + 0.21 + 0.518$
2. $0.75 + 0.01 + 0.88$
3. $0.201 + 0.6 + 0.93$
4. $0.717 + 0.2 + 0.83$
5. $0.1 + 0.101 + 0.07$
6. $0.22 + 0.202 + 0.7$
7. $0.28 + 0.999 + 0.3$
8. $0.12 + 0.584 + 0.6$
9. $0.71 + 0.376 + 0.5$
10. $0.071 + 0.612 + 0.1$

KEEP DECIMAL POINTS UNDER ONE ANOTHER!

Test 9

Subtraction of decimal fractions

Important! Keep the decimal points in line again – and the figures that follow them. See how it works here:

0.761 – 0.343

$$\begin{array}{r} 51 \\ 0.7\cancel{6}\cancel{1} \\ 0.343- \\ \hline 0.418 \\ \hline \end{array}$$

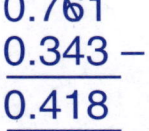

Get the idea? Right! Now try these

1. 0.67 – 0.56
2. 0.41 – 0.18
3. 0.842 – 0.721
4. 0.992 – 0.66
5. 0.391 – 0.222
6. 0.735 – 0.28
7. 0.94 – 0.49
8. 0.603 – 0.321
9. 0.55 – 0.09
10. 0.718 – 0.009

Test 10

Multiplication and division: the jumping dot

- To make a whole number 10 times bigger you add one 0   7 → 70
- 100 times bigger add two 00   7 → 700
- 1000 times bigger add three 000   7 → 7000

WHEN DEALING WITH DECIMAL FRACTIONS YOU JUMP THE POINT INSTEAD

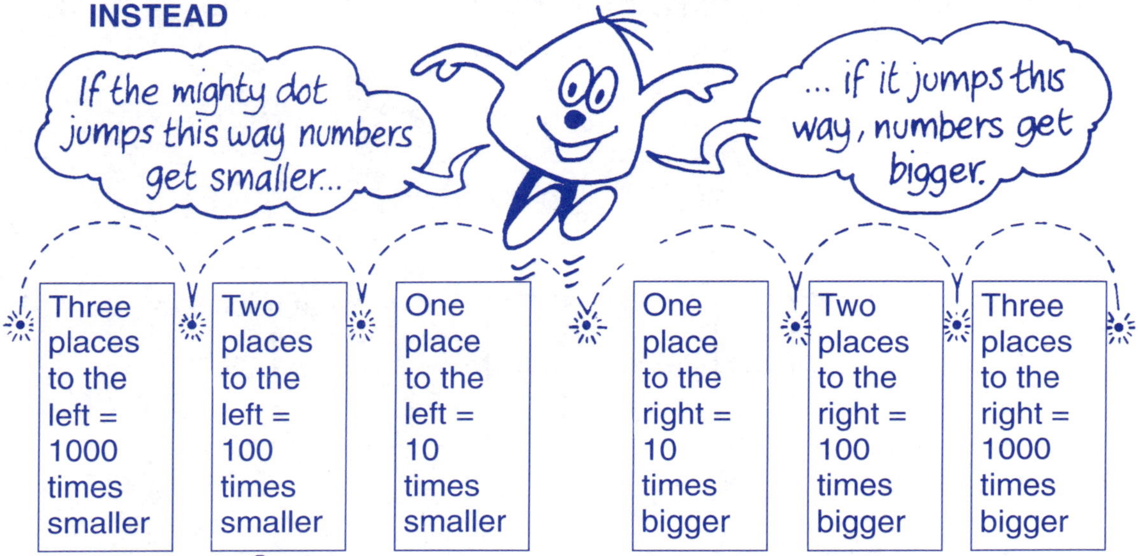

If the mighty dot jumps this way numbers get smaller...

... if it jumps this way, numbers get bigger.

| Three places to the left = 1000 times smaller | Two places to the left = 100 times smaller | One place to the left = 10 times smaller | One place to the right = 10 times bigger | Two places to the right = 100 times bigger | Three places to the right = 1000 times bigger |

Example

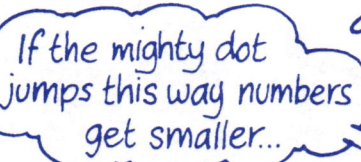

1.32 × 10 = 13.2

1.32 ÷ 10 = 0.132

Now try these:

Add a 0 if there aren't enough figures to jump - as in number 7

1 2.57 × 10 =   2 2.57 ÷ 10 =

3 13.12 × 10 =   4 13.12 ÷ 10 =

5 27.37 × 100 =   6 27.37 ÷ 100 =

7 25.7 × 100 =   8 25.7 ÷ 100 =

9 106.328 × 1000 =   10 106.328 ÷ 1000 =

End-of-book test

To the marker: put a ✔ or a ✘

1 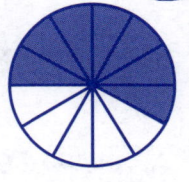 Write the fraction for the part shaded in _____

2 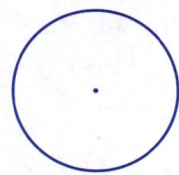 Shade in $\frac{1}{8}$ of this circle

3 A [grid]   What fraction of B is A? _____
   B [grid]

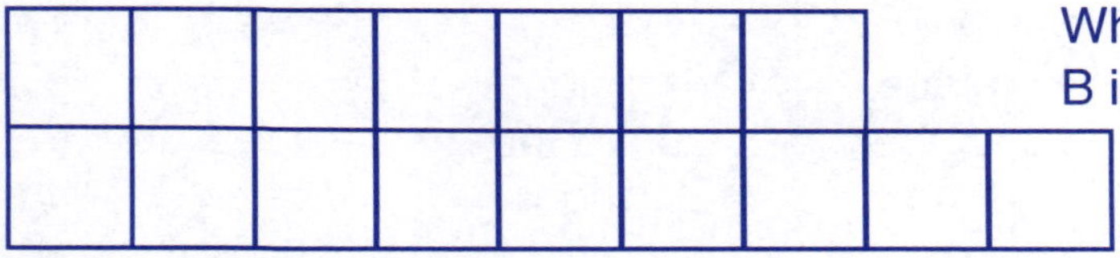

4 Cancel down to lowest terms $\frac{8}{24}$ = _____

5 Put a ring round the odd man out
   $\frac{1}{9}$ $\frac{4}{27}$ $\frac{2}{18}$ $\frac{10}{90}$ $\frac{5}{45}$

6 If a kilo box is a quarter full how many grams does it contain? _____ g

7 [clock face] Draw the hand to show the fraction $\frac{5}{12}$

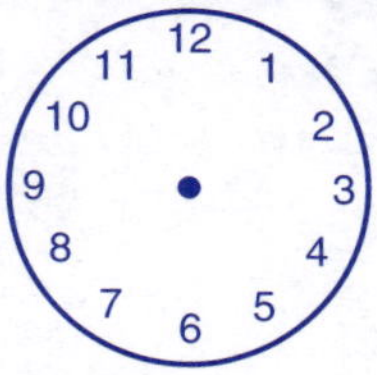

8 $\frac{3}{4} + \frac{1}{5} =$

9 $1\frac{7}{9} + 2\frac{2}{3} =$

10 $\frac{7}{8} - \frac{3}{4} =$

11 $3\frac{2}{3} - \frac{3}{4} =$

12 $\frac{4}{5} \times \frac{5}{6} =$

13 $\frac{5}{12} \div \frac{1}{6} =$

14 How many hundredths? $0.929 =$

15 Convert to ordinary fraction, $0.37 =$

16 Convert to decimal fraction, $\frac{10}{11}$ $= 0.$
    using a calculator.

17 Convert to decimal fraction using conversion line
    on p.24 $\frac{2}{3} = 0.$

18 Express as decimal of £1
        50p + 10p + 5p + 1p = 0.

19 Add these using the number line on p.23
                    $0.7 + 0.9 =$

20 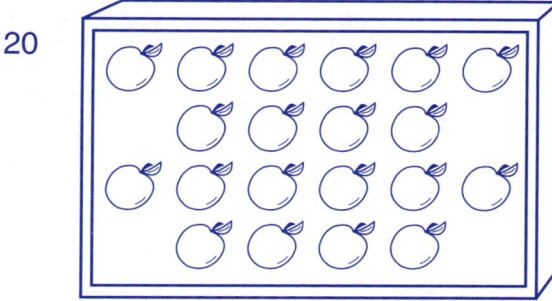   Colour in
                           0.5 of the
                           apples in this box

21 $0.35 + 0.712 + 0.9 =$

22 $0.428 - 0.15 =$

23 $73.42 \times 100 =$

24 $73.42 \div 100 =$

25 If the decimal point jumps three spaces to the right the number
    gets _____ times bigger.
    Write in the missing word

    See how you rate on the chart over the page.

ANSWERS

FRACTIONS
Test 1
(1) $\frac{1}{2}$ (2) $\frac{2}{3}$ (3) $\frac{4}{6}$ (4) $\frac{3}{5}$ (5) $\frac{7}{9}$ (6) $\frac{5}{7}$ (7) $\frac{4}{8}$ (8) $\frac{10}{11}$
(9) $\frac{1}{4}$ (10) $\frac{2}{6}$

Test 2

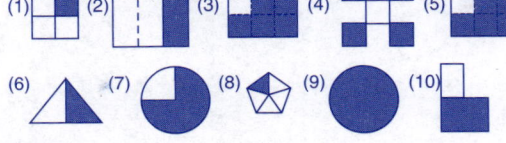

Test 3
(1) $\frac{1}{2}$ (2) $\frac{3}{4}$ (3) $\frac{2}{3}$ (4) $\frac{3}{5}$ (5) $\frac{5}{6}$ (6) $\frac{1}{12}$ (7) $\frac{1}{4}$ (8) $\frac{1}{2}$
(9) $\frac{1}{6}$ (10) $\frac{3}{6}$

Test 4
(1) $\frac{1}{2}$ (2) $\frac{1}{3}$ (3) $\frac{3}{4}$ (4) $\frac{1}{4}$ (5) $\frac{3}{4}$ (6) $\frac{2}{3}$ (7) $\frac{9}{10}$ (8) $\frac{4}{5}$
(9) $\frac{2}{7}$ (10) $\frac{1}{10}$

Test 5
(1) 9 (2) 7 (3) 46p (4) 4 (5) 30 (6) 16 (7) £5
(8) 1 m 40 cm (9) 33 (10) $\frac{1}{10}$

Test 6

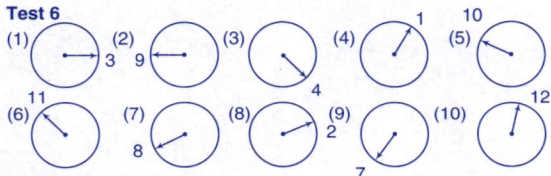

Test 7
(1) $\frac{200}{400}$ (2) $\frac{9}{40}$ (3) $\frac{11}{45}$ (4) $\frac{9}{64}$ (5) $\frac{9}{12}$
(6) $\frac{2}{15}$ (7) $\frac{20}{24}$ (8) $\frac{10}{100}$ (9) $\frac{140}{260}$ (10) $\frac{20}{45}$

Test 8
(1) $\frac{4}{8}$ or $\frac{1}{2}$ (2) $\frac{7}{9}$ (3) $\frac{5}{6}$ (4) $\frac{5}{8}$ (5) $\frac{5}{12}$
(6) $\frac{9}{10}$ (7) $\frac{8}{15}$ (8) $\frac{10}{21}$ (9) $\frac{11}{12}$ (10) $\frac{14}{15}$

Test 9
(1) $1\frac{1}{6}$ (2) $1\frac{1}{8}$ (3) $1\frac{4}{9}$ (4) $1\frac{1}{10}$ (5) $1\frac{3}{12}$ or $1\frac{1}{4}$
(1) $3\frac{4}{5}$ (2) $5\frac{7}{8}$ (3) $4\frac{2}{9}$ (4) $7\frac{1}{6}$ (5) $5\frac{1}{12}$

Test 10
(1) $\frac{1}{5}$ (2) $\frac{1}{2}$ (3) $\frac{3}{8}$ (4) $\frac{1}{3}$ (5) $\frac{3}{14}$ (6) $\frac{5}{16}$ (7) $\frac{9}{40}$ (8) $\frac{11}{21}$
(9) $\frac{1}{24}$ (10) $\frac{7}{20}$

Test 11
(1) $2\frac{2}{3}$ (2) $\frac{3}{4}$ (3) $\frac{7}{8}$ (4) $\frac{5}{6}$ (5) $2\frac{1}{2}$
(6) $1\frac{9}{10}$ (7) $3\frac{3}{4}$ (8) $\frac{2}{3}$ (9) $2\frac{7}{9}$ (10) $4\frac{11}{14}$

Test 12
(1) $\frac{3}{10}$ (2) $\frac{9}{20}$ (3) $\frac{7}{24}$ (4) $\frac{1}{32}$ (5) $\frac{7}{45}$ (6) $\frac{9}{80}$ (7) $\frac{3}{14}$ (8) $\frac{5}{36}$
(9) $\frac{10}{99}$ (10) $\frac{1}{10}$

Test 13
(1) 3 (2) 4 (3) $1\frac{3}{4}$ (4) $2\frac{2}{5}$ (5) 6
(6) $1\frac{1}{14}$ (7) $1\frac{1}{11}$ (8) 5 (9) $2\frac{1}{2}$ (10) 2

DECIMAL FRACTIONS
Test 1
(1) 6 (2) 4 (3) 2 (4) 8 (5) 5 (6) 8 (7) 9
(8) 0 (9) 0 (10) 0

Test 2
(1) £0.12 (2) £0.03 (3) £0.25 (4) £0.51 (5) £0.20
(6) £0.32 (7) £0.65 (8) £0.18 (9) £0.82 (10) £0.37

Test 3
(1) 0.7 (2) 1.2 (3) 1 (4) 0.9 (5) 1.2 (6) 0.8
(7) 1.3 (8) 1.2 (9) 1.7 (10) 1.9

Test 4
(1) 0.3 (2) $\frac{3}{5}$ (3) 0.25 (4) $\frac{3}{4}$ (5) 0.6 (6) $\frac{2}{5}$
(7) 0.8 (8) $\frac{7}{10}$ (9) 0.33 (10) $\frac{1}{5}$

Test 5
(1) colour in one of the four sections (2) 50 cm = 500 mm
(3) colour in seven stars (4) draw three more packets (5) 0.7
(6) 0.1 (7) 9 (8) 1 m 50 cm (9) 80p (10) 999

Test 6
(1) $\frac{7}{10}$ (2) $\frac{26}{100} = \frac{13}{50}$ (3) $\frac{18}{100} = \frac{9}{50}$ (4) $\frac{1}{10}$ (5) $\frac{78}{100} = \frac{39}{50}$
(6) $\frac{216}{1000} = \frac{27}{125}$ (7) $\frac{35}{100} = \frac{7}{20}$ (8) $\frac{8}{10} = \frac{4}{5}$ (9) $\frac{377}{1000}$ (10) $\frac{9}{1000}$

Test 7
(1) 0.25 (2) 0.625 (3) 0.45 (4) 0.666 (5) 0.111
(6) 0.833 (7) 0.875 (8) 0.2727 (9) 0.95 (10) 0.8181

Test 8
(1) 1.028 (2) 1.64 (3) 1.731 (4) 1.747 (5) 0.271
(6) 1.122 (7) 1.579 (8) 1.304 (9) 1.586 (10) 0.783

Test 9
(1) 0.11 (2) 0.23 (3) 0.121 (4) 0.332 (5) 0.169
(6) 0.455 (7) 0.45 (8) 0.282 (9) 0.46 (10) 0.709

Test 10
(1) 25.7 (2) 0.257 (3) 131.2 (4) 1.312 (5) 2737
(6) 0.2737 (7) 2570 (8) 0.257 (9) 106328
(10) 0.106328

END-OF-BOOK TEST
(1) $\frac{7}{12}$ (2) (3) $\frac{7}{9}$ (4) $\frac{1}{3}$ (5) $\frac{4}{27}$ (6) 250 g

(7) (8) $\frac{19}{20}$ (9) $4\frac{4}{9}$ (10) $\frac{1}{8}$ (11) $2\frac{11}{12}$ (12) $\frac{2}{3}$

(13) $2\frac{1}{2}$ (14) 2 (15) $\frac{37}{100}$ (16) 0.9090 (17) 0.66

(18) £0.66 (19) 1.6 (20) colour in 10 (21) 1.962

(22) 0.278 (23) 7342 (24) 0.7342

(25) a thousand (1000)

HOW MANY STARS?			
	*	**	***
Age 9 or below	5 – 10	11 – 16	17 +
Age 10 – 11	8 – 12	13 – 18	19 +